WHO TOLD YOU THAT YOU WERE NAKED?

2024

You are fearfully and wonderfully made Ps 139:14

[signature] Papeczki

Romans 1:16

WHO TOLD YOU THAT YOU WERE NAKED?

How to walk on top of the oceans of shame

EVERETT POPE

XULON PRESS

Xulon Press
555 Winderley Pl, Suite 225
Maitland, FL 32751
407.339.4217
www.xulonpress.com

© 2024 by Everett Pope

All rights reserved solely by the author. The author guarantees all contents are original and do not infringe upon the legal rights of any other person or work. No part of this book may be reproduced in any form without the permission of the author.

Due to the changing nature of the Internet, if there are any web addresses, links, or URLs included in this manuscript, these may have been altered and may no longer be accessible. The views and opinions shared in this book belong solely to the author and do not necessarily reflect those of the publisher. The publisher therefore disclaims responsibility for the views or opinions expressed within the work.

Unless otherwise indicated, Scripture quotations taken from the New King James Version (NKJV). Copyright © 1982 by Thomas Nelson, Inc. Used by permission. All rights reserved.

Paperback ISBN-13: 978-1-66289-463-3
eBook ISBN-13: 978-1-66289-464-0

Acknowledgements

This book is dedicated to my wife Myra, and my family. By family, I mean my two sons, my parents, my brothers and my sister. I mean all of my nephews and nieces. I mean my church family. A special shout out to Neveah Carrington, an awesome encouragement to me in this process. There are so many people that encouraged me along the way to bring this work to fruition. A special thanks to my brother Timotheus Pope for helping in the editing process. If this work is helpful and flows it is because of his creative contribution. I am very grateful for everyone God has used in my life and in this process to make this dream of mine a reality.

This book will take you on a journey of personal transformation. I will show you how to overcome your fears, overcome your limitations and overcome your shame. I will show you how to live a healthy and happy life without succumbing to the pitfalls of shame.

Contents

Chapter 1: THE QUESTION: Who Told You, You Were Naked? 1

Chapter 2: Echos of Shame Shame Shame 6

Chapter 3: A Description of Shame 12

Chapter 4: The Whispering Voices of Shame 19

Chapter 5: Calluses from Masks of Shame 24

Chapter 6: Crossing the Oceans - Empowered by Shame 28

Chapter 7: Liberation through Vulnerability 31

Chapter 8: Shame & Short Circuits 38

Chapter 9: Haunted by False Humility 41

Chapter 10: Family Call - Who Told Me I Was Naked? 45

Chapter 11: The Fight: The Answer to the Question 31

Chapter 12: CAUTION: Willpower Is Not Always on Will Call ... 56

Chapter 13: Shame Shame Go Away - Empty Your Cup 63

Conclusion: 70

Introduction:

I am a basketball junkie. I love the game. I love playing the game. I enjoy debating who is the greatest of all time? One day, I was in Lowes and ran across a friendly couple. I knew their faces. They were the parents of an old basketball friend of mine that I had played basketball with and had some great conversations. To my amazement, they shared that he passed away from a fentanyl overdose. Obviously, I was immediately saddened, and my entire countenance changed right there in the middle of Lowes. There are so many ways people are being lured into destructive habits I thought. I experienced a range of emotions right there in the aisle with the charcoal and grills where a fire was lit inside of me. We had an awkward moment for sure, then in the awkwardness of the moment, I expressed my condolences. But, I knew this was more than a random opportunity for compassion and empathy. This was a God encounter. I had just left my office at the church property where I am the Pastor and went over to Lowe's to purchase 84 pieces of cement pavers when I ran into this lovely couple. I was not expecting this, but Yes I am sure of it, God was at work.

Next, the father of my friend asked me a question, "What is the most important question in the Bible?" Wow! To be honest, several answers crossed my mind. I have been a pastor for almost two decades. I was raised and trained by a Pastor, my dad. I love the Bible and have no shame in letting you know that this book charts a journey that is filled with Biblical references. However, I wasn't entirely sure how to best answer his question. As I was pondering how to answer him, he answered his own question. "Who told you

you were naked?" Interestingly enough, this question was the exact title of the book I was in the process of writing from Genesis 3:11. I knew then the Lord was nudging me to finish the work He had placed inside of my heart. This book is the finished work that charts my journey from shame to victory and freedom. May it become a small part of your journey to wholeness, wellness and peace. I have prayed for you that this book is not a mere read but an experience to share with others as it chronicles my own terrible bout with shame. I love when Peter asked Jesus if he could come to him on the water (Matthew 14:28). Peter walked on water for at least a moment. This is a very useful analogy to what this book is intended to motivate you to become. I want you to be able to walk in freedom on top of the waters of shame and guilt just as God has taught me. But first, you must get out of the boat. So, let's take a look at the origin of this question. Hang on and enjoy the ride!

Chapter 1:

THE QUESTION: Who Told You, You Were Naked?

11 And He said, "Who told you that you were naked? Have you eaten from the tree of which I commanded you that you should not eat?" (Genesis 3:11)

11 וַיֹּאמֶר מִי הִגִּיד לְךָ כִּי עֵירֹם אָתָּה הֲמִן־הָעֵץ אֲשֶׁר צִוִּיתִיךָ לְבִלְתִּי אֲכָל־מִמֶּנּוּ אָכָלְתָּ׃

Who told you that you were naked? This question comes within the first three chapters of the first book in the Bible. It's the question that brought life to this Book. The narrative in Genesis, our word which means " beginning," starts with the creation of all things, including humanity. God created a perfect world where humans were completely innocent, but given the opportunity to choose a life other than innocence. God created two trees that He put in the middle of the Garden of Eden. One was called the Tree of Knowledge and the other was called the Tree of Life. God gave total freedom to eat from every tree in the Garden, but forbade that humans would eat from the Tree of Knowledge because on the day they would eat of it, they would surely die. It was beautiful and the Garden was perfect, but then something went terribly, terribly wrong.

1 Now the serpent was more cunning than any beast of the field which the LORD God had made. And he said to the

> woman, "Has God indeed said, 'You shall not eat of every tree of the garden'?" 2 And the woman said to the serpent, "We may eat the fruit of the trees of the garden; 3 but of the fruit of the tree which is in the midst of the garden, God has said, 'You shall not eat it, nor shall you touch it, lest you die.'"

Havah or Eve as we call her, the mother of all living, opens our great drama of life speaking with a snake. Perhaps the origin of our mythical dragon. Now the Bible tells us that this was not just any ordinary snake. According to Revelation 12:9

> So the great dragon was cast out, **that serpent of old**, called the Devil and Satan, who deceives the whole world; he was cast to the earth, and his angels were cast out with him.

The Apostle John refers back to Genesis in Revelation and reveals the true culprit that is entertaining Eve in the garden. This is the arch enemy of God and God's people. He is often called Satan which means adversary.

> 4 Then the serpent said to the woman, "You will not surely die. 5 For God knows that in the day you eat of it your eyes will be opened, and you will be like God, knowing good and evil." 6 So when the woman saw that the tree was good for food, that it was pleasant to the eyes, and a tree desirable to make one wise, she took of its fruit and ate. She also gave to her husband with her, and he ate. 7 Then the eyes of both of them were opened, and they knew that they were naked; and they sewed fig leaves together and made themselves coverings. 8 And they heard the sound of the LORD God walking in the garden in the cool of the day, and Adam and his wife hid themselves from the presence of the LORD God among the trees of the garden.

This next section is where the story picks up and we see the age old question.

> *9 Then the LORD God called to Adam and said to him, "Where are you?" 10 So he said, "I heard Your voice in the garden, and I was afraid because I was naked; and I hid myself." 11 And He said, "Who told you that you were naked? (Genesis 3:1-11a NKJ)*

BOOM! Shame entered the world the moment Adam disobeyed God. This trembling feeling of failure and insecurity arrived at the exact same time when a curiosity was met and a command was broken. This curiosity led to disobedience. The consequences of disobedience were disastrous then, and they still are. Shame is one of those consequences. Shame is the idea that something is frighteningly wrong with me. It is a self-conscious feeling of unease or awkwardness. It is a looming discomfort of mind. Adam and Eve were so ashamed of their nakedness that they covered themselves with fig leaves. Whenever we experience shame, we often feel the need to cover up. We feel we need protection. We cover ourselves with carefully crafted fig leaves. The process seems to start over each time we disobey. I want you to keep in mind, guilt is the idea that a line has been crossed or a standard has been broken. Shame, however, focuses attention on identity, It attacks our very idea of ourselves. Therefore shame reinforces our guilt. Shame follows up to tell us we are not who we are supposed to be. God's question to the first humans shares deep insight into how shame works and how we can prove mastery over this sinister villain. The question, by the way, that God asked "Who told you that you were naked?", brings awareness to something deeper. Shame perverts what was once innocent. My experience with shame concludes that it begs for a way out of the feelings of embarrassment. Cloak me! Cope for me! Medicate me! Please silence those condemning thoughts in my head that tell me I am the problem! The question was "Who told you that you were naked?" Notice the follow up question

Have you eaten from the tree of which I commanded you that you should not eat?" (Genesis 3:11b)

In other words, what has happened inside of you to make you aware of what you should not know? What caused you to embrace an illusion, a mere shadow of what is actually true?

A friend of our family went with us to fellowship at our local church from time to time. Like many, he was mischievous for sure, but far from a menace to society. One Sunday morning we heard some very bad news through the grapevine, and as you know, bad news travels faster than a toddler to the toy section at Walmart. Our friend, let's call him Sam, was in trouble. He had been shot that previous night. Not only had Sam been shot, but we were told that the wound was fatal. It was a horrible moment when I thought of my last words with him. I had just talked with him one week prior to this heart wrenching news. Suddenly, I was prompted to call his cell phone. To my surprise, Sam answered the phone! Not only was he still alive, he had not been shot at all. He was relieved to know that he was alive and, obviously, I was as well. I wanted to know who had spread this atrocious rumor. Who started this narrative that Sam was fatally wounded by a gunshot? Who lied to us and made us feel such sorrow? Upon hearing the good news of the truth that he was still alive and had NOT been shot, I went from sad and angry to relieved and then overjoyed. As you continue reading, I pray your experience is similar as you uncover the truth by turning the pages of this book.

REFLECTION:

What are some areas that you have experienced shame?

Reflect on a time when you were in a situation where something was being reported about you that was not true? How did you feel?

Do you agree that shame accompanies disobedience? Why? Or Why not?

Chapter 2:

Echos of Shame, Shame Shame

I had the privilege to go to Israel and stand in a place where most likely Jesus actually stood. It is the place that is known for his famous sermon on the mount. You can read the entire sermon in about 18 minutes and it is found in the book of Matthew, chapters five through seven. While on this hilly terrain which looks like a natural made amphitheater, I naturally did what most people would attempt. I projected my voice and quickly experienced how Jesus could speak to thousands of people without our modern technology.

There was no portable public address (PA) system, but you could hear my voice echo into the distance. It was quite remarkable. This is how the feelings involved with my shame reverberated throughout my soul. Shame is like an echo billowing over and over again. It is there, in my subconscious, condemning me, telling me something is wrong, that I am not good enough, and that I just need to do better. No one is celebrating you in this life it bellows. Shame can affect how we experience our emotions. Emotions have a physiological component. The component is what we call the feeling flowing from the emotion. The emotion is the energy in motion and what happens in the physical body is what we call our feelings or sensations that accompany that energy. Each emotion manifests within the body, and can look a lot of different ways. My experience was that shame would cause me to believe things that would block appropriate emotional responses and delay my feelings. The lingering result was that lies became my truth and caused my emotions and feelings to adjust to that false narrative.

It stands to reason that prior to the fall of humanity there would be no need for shame because the world was perfect. Therefore, I believe this feeling developed once the first couple ate from the fruit of the tree of the knowledge of good and evil. As the text says, their eyes were opened, and they knew they were naked. Before we go any further, it is important to note that shame is also not always a bad thing. It can be used to motivate in positive ways and yield positive results. Paul says to the Thessalonians that shame would be used to bring a wandering follower back to his senses.

> *And if anyone does not obey our word in this epistle, note that person and do not keep company with him, that he may be ashamed. (2 Thessalonians 2:14)*

However, if it is true that shame came after the fall, then it does derive from our emotions, which came at creation. Our emotions were given to us by God that we might understand where we are internally and where we stand on stage in this play called life. Our emotions are not to lead us, but they are data to help us navigate our current reality and get back on track when we are off. Emotions help us establish rhythms and standards. Emotions make us aware of what is happening on the inside. Emotions are more like the thermometer of our well-being. Our emotions measure the flow of happiness. Unlike a thermostat which sets and controls the climate in a room, our emotions do not control us; they only reveal to us our state of being more like a thermometer. We should not make decisions based purely on our emotions. However our emotions can help us in decision making. Our emotions receive and send signals to the body, causing us to feel certain things in certain ways. We are to assess the cause and circumstances behind our emotions and our feelings. We are to evaluate consequences for each decision we make. How many possible outcomes exist for each choice that is made? Shame can be used for good; but, for the sake of the journey ahead of us, I am referencing the shadow side or negative side of shame used to mask our true self.

> *When pride comes, then comes shame; But with the humble is wisdom (Proverbs 11:2).*

Shame promotes a feeling of deep personal humiliation and disgrace, namely a sense of unworthiness. In Proverbs 11, we are made aware of the true culprit and root cause of our shame. The narrator of our shame is pride. Pride is the voice of shame. Pride can be viewed as a self-estimate of ourselves. Confidence and true self esteem come from established humility not misplaced pride. This proverb gives us the true understanding that shame is birthed from pride. How can you have a true understanding of what you look like inside without a standard to mirror? James uses a mirror as a metaphor for the Scriptures. God gives us the truth whereby we can have a correct inner perspective.

> *23 For if anyone is a hearer of the word and not a doer, he is like a man observing his natural face in a mirror; 24 for he observes himself, goes away, and immediately forgets what kind of man he was. 25 But he who looks into the perfect law of liberty and continues in it, and is not a forgetful hearer but a doer of the work, this one will be blessed in what he does. (James 1:23-25)*

We tend to overestimate or underestimate our true potential. Pride occurs when this estimation of self either produces a higher sense of the self ahead of others or reduces oneself to a lower position in one's own eyes. This estimation can work in many different ways, as it is a deception. That's why shame is so elusive, making it difficult to trace or discover its root. Therefore, addressing this subtle weapon of great destruction is not simply humbling oneself. In fact, dogged discipline would also fall short in tackling shame. The only answer is expressing humility. Humility is a true estimation of self-value and worth. Understanding how pride and shame work together is how we begin to defeat the core lies and ask the question: Who told you that you were naked? Who told you that you were not good enough? We can even overestimate the value of relationships, like friendships or authorities in our lives. We give power to those people to create deep wounds and frightening scars. What made our shame narrative so believable? How is it that we allow ourselves to be overcome by shame? The answer may shock you. Being able to name and describe our emotions and feelings provides us with the opportunity to understand ourselves and our reactions. It is paramount to be able to reflect. Understanding the ramifications of our own emotions, enables us to empathize as we begin to understand the emotional experience of others when they encounter us and our shame. Peter Fonagy discusses this in his work on "mentailization." He believes this understanding is crucial to the ability to empathize and mentalize with others. Mentalization is the ability to understand the mental state of oneself or others. This is an essential part of healthy relationships. Let's look at four emotions expressed in Scripture. I use these as a basis for understanding emotions.

1. Joy: the energy of excitement because something needs to be celebrated.

   You will show me the path of life; In Your presence is fullness of joy; At Your right hand are pleasures forevermore. (Psalm 16:11)

2. Grief: the energy of loss because something is missing and different than before.

And the LORD was sorry that He had made man on the earth, and He was grieved in His heart. (Genesis 6:6)

3. Anger: the energy of justice because something is not the way it should be.

34 "And the LORD heard the sound of your words, and was angry, and took an oath, saying, 35 'Surely not one of these men of this evil generation shall see that good land of which I swore to give to your fathers, 36 except Caleb the son of Jephunneh; he shall see it, and to him and his children I am giving the land on which he walked, because he wholly followed the LORD.' 37 The LORD was also angry with me for your sakes, saying, 'Even you shall not go in there. (Deuteronomy 1:34-37)

4. Fear: the energy of danger because something is unsafe or unknown.

"And do not fear those who kill the body but cannot kill the soul. But rather fear Him who is able to destroy both soul and body in hell. (Matthew 10:28)

My wife has had to fight through shame and disappointment in her life. Myra was teased in school. I love my wife. She is such a blessing to me. There is no way that I could have written this book without her. Nor could I have written this book without some of our very own stories. I have her permission to use her story to illustrate again how shame renders us powerless. My wife was born with an acute lung problem. Her father was murdered at the age of four. She battled with health issues from the beginning. She underwent a major surgery when she was eleven years old. This also caused her to undergo a series of radiation treatments. When she went to middle school she was tortured by the little rascal students. I am sure you know just how cruel teens can be. As a result of her radiation treatments, she had lost most of her hair. In her opinion, she was only a sight for sore eyes. They laughed at her and called her names. You can imagine the shame she felt. Her self esteem was on an all time low. There is no way she should have survived the emotional bullying, but she did. She survived the lung surgery. She survived the radiation treatments. She survived the teasing. She recovered. She soon blossomed into an attractive young lady. She was the envy of those who had ridiculed her in her darkest moments. She had victory and healing. She had friends and family who rallied around her to encourage her and support her. However, she did not at that time survive or overcome the shame her scars from surgery left her. She became bitter. The scars from her life experiences, at that point in her life, left her fully ashamed and distant. She learned to survive and cope. She was functional but she was broken. Her emotions were hijacked and rearranged. Your emotions were given to you to assess your soul's sensitivity to certain stimuli. They are not given to us to make decisions. They are there to help us understand, not to inform us of what actions to take. I don't know about you, but I love martial arts. Shame is like a stealthy ninja. This stealthy ninja is able to hide and is willing to strike in the darkness without a moment's notice. It has in its arsenal an entire array of weapons used to paralyze its victims. Survival tactics never translate to freedom.

REFLECTIONS

What are some of your insecurities?

How do you feel when you hear the word victim?

How do you feel when you hear the word victory?

What feelings have you encountered that may have come from shame?

Chapter 3:

A Description of Shame

Webster's dictionary defines shame as a painful emotion caused by consciousness of guilt, shortcoming, or failure. There are two acronyms that are sometimes used for shame: (1) Should Have Already Mastered Everything and, (2) Should Have Already Made Excuses. Shame can generate emotions mentioned earlier. Shame can lead to anger. Shame can lead to grief. Shame can lead to fear. Shame can lead to an expression of happiness. Think about it. Imagine you are asked to do something that you are competent of but low self esteem or anxiety has crippled your effectiveness. As you contemplate whether or not to accept the offer, someone less competent volunteers and you experience relief. Dare I say, a sense of happiness in that moment of relief. Yet, your potential remains untapped as the full expression of who you were meant to be is covered by new "fig leaves." Notice here I used happiness and not joy. Biblically, joy is an emotion expressed as pleasure, peace and contentment that comes from something inside versus something outside. Scripture reminds us of this in James.

> *My brethren, count it all joy when you fall into various trials, (James 1:2)*

Dealing with the core lies created by shame and developing new habits will lead to freedom. We must demand the opportunity to debrief the events of our lives and to make sense of our experiences. Trauma has happened to all of us. Unfortunately, trauma affects us all at different times and in various ways. Trauma as duly noted by the mental health community is not merely what happens to us. It is more so what happens inside of us. We are not entirely sure when the feelings associated with what we experienced will be addressed. Much like a wound, there is a process to healing that takes time. What has happened inside of us must also be healed. Often the coping mechanism of shame is to cover up and quiet the cries of the trauma that brought on the shame. Addictions, overcompensation and even social withdrawal act as medication to mask the shame and numb the pain. This silencing of the lambs has led to much more horror than any motion picture could portray. And yet, there is still an opportunity for victory and solution to what you have been experiencing and feeling due to shame. We must believe that it is not only possible to heal, but that healing is available to us and it is FOR us. Recovery requires a diagnosis in order to be treated, so we must be able to recognize shame when we see it. We are in this together. Don't stop! After all, a problem well described is a problem half solved. I am writing and sharing my experience for your joy and freedom.

> *Not that we have dominion over your faith, but are fellow workers for your joy; for by faith you stand. (2 Corinthians 1:24)*

To experience the true joy that awaits a life that has victory over shame, we must revisit what caused the shame, just as a doctor revisits symptoms to diagnose an illness.

> *Remember: When pride comes, then comes shame; But with the humble is wisdom. (Proverbs 11:2)*

All of us are born with imperfections. In this life we learn how to live with those imperfections. However, what is most unsatisfying often is finding out how others respond to our imperfections. I have spent so much time trying to figure out how to please the people around me. I thought love for me was based on the acceptance of others and their acceptance was directly correlated to my performance. At times, although I would not have said it this way before, if others could be pleased with me, it would be easier for me to be pleased with myself. In fact, I remember a time when I went with a friend of mine to the pool. I could not swim. My friend asked me if I could, and I lied, "sure I can swim." I went to the deep end and I jumped off the diving board having no clue how to swim. I jumped as far as I could jump. As a matter of fact, I jumped from what was 10 ft all the way to the 4 ft section where I knew I could stand up. Believe me when I hit the water, I was paddling for my life literally. I thought I would die, but if I am to be honest with you, I also thought drowning would have been much better AND much easier than facing the truth that I couldn't swim. Everyone else could swim. I was the **only** one who couldn't swim. No one had taught **me** how to swim. I felt left out, abandoned, and **alone**. There I was, the oddball who couldn't swim. Maybe you resonate with me. I am not going to teach you how to swim but I do want to keep you from drowning in shame. I want to help you tread these waters and overcome those who impose their own value and worth upon others. These values that are created externally present opportunities for fig leaves which are bad for swimming. In fact, wearing those fig leaves makes it easier to drown. How we view our own story reinforces the shame we experience while entertaining the thought of being discovered or exposed. That word even dredges up sensations of vulnerability and weakness, frailty and embarrassment. In the pages ahead I invite you to join me. We will cognitively reframe the narrative of our life experiences in a way that allows you to walk on top of the oceans of your shame. It always helps to know you are not alone.

Moses was a powerful Bible hero, a hero that struggled with shame. Perhaps his shame started when he recognized he was an adopted

Hebrew child being raised in an Egyptian palace. In fact, we hear in Genesis 43:32 and 46:34 that the Egyptians would not even eat with the Hebrews and despised shepherds. Can you imagine what Moses might have heard about the Hebrews, his people, growing up in Pharaoh's house?

Imagine growing up in a home, being raised by an ethnic people that have enslaved and considered your ethnicity as a whole an abomination. When he was grown, he went out to his people to check on them. Perhaps Moses had a survivor's guilt. One day, he saw an Egyptian beating a Hebrew and he "looked this way and that way, and when he saw no one, he killed the Egyptian and hid him in the sand," (Exodus 2:12). Think about why he might have looked "this way and that way," and why he did not move until he knew no one was looking. I'm guessing there was a little shame present even in doing the thing he figured was best at that moment. The next day when he went out and saw two Hebrew brothers fighting each other, he intervened and asked them why they were fighting. They rejected him and let him know that they knew his little secret. In verse 15, we find that his own surrogate grandfather planned to kill him, so he ran away and he hid. Sound familiar? Moses had a lot of reasons to live in shame. Yet, this same Moses is arguably the greatest prophet in Israel's history. He had unique encounters with God. One encounter that is unlike any encounter that anyone else has had in Bible history. He experienced the presence of God through a bush that was burning but not consumed. It was a spectacular miracle. God spoke to Moses from the bush and gave him orders that troubled Moses greatly. Moses, who was to free the people of Israel after 400 years of slavery, was battling. I wonder if he thought, "Are you kidding, I couldn't even stop two Hebrews from fighting and you want me to convince Pharaoh to let them all go?!" God gave him an incredible feat to accomplish. However, Moses emphasized his inadequacy and inability to fulfill

God's command because of an insecurity about his speech. His shame was reinforced and empowered by low self-esteem. Imagine that with me for just a moment. Israel's greatest prophet had the greatest weakness you could imagine for a public speaker. Moses even said," Lord please send someone else." (Exodus 6:13). Moses was speaking to God. Can you see evidence of shame in the words of Moses? He clearly didn't understand who God really was at that time. He didn't understand that God was omniscient and knew all. The beautiful piece about this story is that God chose to use Moses with all of his frailties and insecurities. I suppose the most wonderful thing about this passage is, if there was hope for Moses there is hope for us. God knew every fear Moses had and the shame, yet he still chose to use Moses. God loves using broken vessels. In fact, God reprimanded Moses for highlighting his inadequacies, gently reminding Moses of a simple truth, " He (God) had made man's mouth," (Exodus 4:11).

He knew that Moses had a speech impediment, but that was not going to stop God from inviting him into a space of intimacy and collaboration. God knew something Moses didn't know, and what we may not recognize. Our shame will paralyze us if we don't find the confidence to move beyond it and to do what is best. God told Moses that he's going to send Aaron, Moses's brother, because Aaron is a good speaker. The idea is God wanted to use Moses. I might add right now that God also wants to use you. Early in this text in Exodus 34, God asked Moses, "what is in your hand?" Moses replied, "A rod." (Exodus 4:2). God told Moses to put it on the ground. God used the rod. It miraculously turned into a serpent. I don't know if that's what God will do with your ink pen or your hair brush or comb. Most of us would be freaked out if He did but I must ask the question to you: what is that in your hand? Think about it. God used an ordinary rod to do extraordinary work in the midst of calling an ordinary man to an extraordinary work. If God could use the rod, then God could certainly use Moses. In fact, God is willing to use anything that we make available to him to include people, objects, animals, dreams, etc. This truth is illustrated in my favorite Christmas song: The Little Drummer Boy. In the aftermath of a child born in a stable there stands this little boy with nothing to offer the King except for his ability to play a drum. Yet he is determined to play his drum for the Lord. Shame cannot stop us from doing what God is calling us to do. James Earl Jones, the great voice of Darth Vader also had a speech impediment. Shame did not stop him and it did not stop Moses. Let's apply our question to Moses' situation. Who told you that you couldn't speak well? Or who told you that as a result of the way you speak God could not use you? Shame says you should be able to do this but you can't. It taunts, how dare you attempt to do this feat that is far beyond your capacity, ability, and potential? You will be embarrassed, you will make a fool out of yourself, you'll be the laughingstock of the community. I'm sure shame said to Moses, 'Look at you. You can't speak. You're not even really a Hebrew, are you? You are by birth, but not by experience. You don't have a shared Hebrew experience. They won't accept you. You're a murderer and a coward. Shame thickens around us like a dark rain cloud. The emotion may be fear (am I safe?) and the feeling is often expressed as anxiety. It may be anger (is this right or fair?) and the feeling is expressed as frustration or rage. It could be grief (what am I missing?) and the feeling is expressed as sadness. But, that feeling begins to empower other forms of shameful creativity. If we are not careful, we wallow in that place of darkness. I can see Moses becoming a prolific writer and we know he wrote the Pentateuch (the first five books of the Bible). Yet God wanted to use him to speak to the Pharaoh and to the people. Moses was prompted with a command to face his inadequacies with God at the helm. We need to know that we're in good company, because there are people that God used mightily while still suffering from the impact of their shame. That was not the end of their stories. It is not going to be the end of yours either, especially now that you can begin to recognize shame. It is possible to understand shame and heal.

REFLECTIONS

Which of the following describes you best right now: being defensive (defending yourself), deflective (blaming others), or being definitive (taking responsibility)?

Reflect on a time when you were in a situation like Moses where you felt led to do something that seemed bigger than your capacity, ability, or potential to accomplish the task?

If we were to diagnose shame in your life, what might be some symptoms?

What are some events that have occurred in your life that might be reasons for shame?

Chapter 4:

The Whispering Voices of Shame

When we experience shame on a frequent basis, whether we like it or not, shame begins to drive some of the energy set in motion for us each day. My point is that shame is causing the occurrence of the emotion that causes you to feel some kind of way. In other words, instead of us experiencing the natural process of our thoughts generating an energy based upon an experience, shame is putting energy in motion. It short circuits our natural emotional process and causes us to feel ways that are inconsistent with some of our thoughts. We begin to prejudge the situations around us based upon how shame has rebooted our cognitive process to feel fear where there should be joy or grief where there should be anger. Remember my pool story? Shame caused a confident energy when there should have been much more grief or fear. The need to be approved signaled a joy of sorts, when it certainly should have energized me to grief about not being able to swim or fear that the deep waters of the pool were not safe for a non-swimmer. As a person who has suffered from the tyranny of shame, we will often unintentionally project our process upon others so they experience something similar in relation to us. We may not know it, but shame often causes us to believe others have certain views of us that they have never verbalized. Shame promotes the narrative that may or may not even be true through whispering voices. I have a good friend who frequently says that truth should always overcome our feelings. This saying, like so many other sayings, is much easier said than done. It is difficult to take what we have felt every day and ignore, suppress, or act in direct opposition to the feeling. Yet many times and in many cases this is the very action that should be applied. Once we recognize shame as a driving force, we must address it with what we know to be true. In fact, if we address it we will find ourselves acting in the direct opposite of how we feel. Shame will cause us to stay quiet when we should speak up or speak up when we should stay quiet. It will make us not go after what may be ours, and it'll cause us to shrink back when maybe we should take a stand. It can make us passive when we should be assertive, and overbearing when we should relax. The feelings prompted by shame are not always backed by fact. That feeling can keep us from doing the things that we need to get done and cause us to succeed at the wrong things. Shame also can create the false narrative that we don't deserve something, and can make us feel entitled at the same time. Shame whispers in support of creating a new identity. Shame will create that persona at church, through social media, at school, in the supermarket and at work. Shame repeats the consistent message that our current identity is not helping us. As a matter of fact, it is hurting us. Time for new fig leaves, and maybe a new place to hide. This sentiment is what shame whispers to our heart.

Notice between the "h" and the "t" of "heart" is the word, "ear." Also notice that if you drop the "t" of the word "heart" you are left with the word "hear." It is amazing to me at least that it is hard to get people to hear our heart when the combination of letters is so close. Various voices can contribute to feelings of shame, such as societal expectations, family influences, and personal insecurities. The peer pressure created in our Western world is similar to a pandemic. I remember when I was growing up in the 70's and 80's. The latest dress styles and fads were worn by a few and popularized by our favorite entertainers. Today that pressure is exponential in its impact due to the rise of the internet, social media, and streaming services. There could be someone literally halfway around the world influencing you or your family members right now. Do you want to have an IG blue check? Do you want more followers or subscribers? Sometimes we hear the reverse psychology from shame. Do you want to be alone for the rest of your life? Do you want to be one of those people who never experiences life? I have news for you. If you never experienced the action that shame is calling life you will also never experience the consequences of those reckless actions. For example, if you never drink you will never become an alcoholic. If you don't carry a handgun you will never kill anyone with a handgun. There are many illustrations. Every illustration is a source of offense for one and celebration for another. Our backgrounds are a great place to start when looking for the answer to our question. Who told you that you were naked? Who told you that you would never amount to anything? I have the privilege to serve as a volunteer for a Christian organization called Fellowship of Christian Athletes (FCA). I have met some wonderful people over the years. I have also heard countless stories of shame. One story in particular stands out to me of an athlete, a long- distance runner. She came across her unique skill by running miles to get away from her home environment. A member of her family told her that she would never amount to anything. She is currently married, a graduate with multiple degrees and a smile big as the state of Texas. That family member sure was wrong. However, it took all of this young lady's life to get to a place where she embraced her true identity through her faith. She knew who had lied to her. She refused to allow this declaration from ignorance to become a life sentence for her. She learned to walk on top of the waters of shame, guilt, and humiliation. She knew who she was and who she wanted to be. She fought the good fight and came out on top as a winner. There is no doubt that these voices echoed and whispered in her mind. These voices create a powerful chorus that echoes within the mind of those terrorized by shame. Yes, the words and treatment in her life deeply affected her. Shame escorted her into moments of depression, but she never gave up. The narrative had to be changed. The lie had to be exchanged for the truth. There are strategies for identifying and challenging these negative voices. One strategy that is particularly effective is reclaiming your own narrative. What if we were able to silence that echoing voice and consistent whisper? What if we were able to override those feelings steered by guilt and shame? How much would you pay to have the feeling of unworthiness, guilt or embarrassment erased? What would you give to press forward and to do what needs to be done? What could you accomplish if you found a way to walk on top of your shame? If you found a way to take the shameful, hidden things of your heart, expose them and dispose of them, you could walk triumphantly in recovery. You would not just walk triumphantly in spite of those feelings of inadequacy and discomfort; but, address the true root cause, experiencing the freedom you desperately desire. Freedom, that has a nice ring to it doesn't it? Do you want to be free? You must identify the voices. That is a part of the treatment, once you diagnose the illness of shame. You also must analyze whether the claims are true or false. That's what this book is about: it's about taking those feelings and turning them into motivation for freedom. A self-emancipation proclamation is on the horizon. Let's explore together how I learned to walk on top of the waters of shame. It is time to take off the mask and let freedom ring.

REFLECTION:

What are some projections you have placed on others?

Name some beliefs you hold that others have of you that you have never confirmed.

Reflect on a time when you felt judged by someone who had not directly addressed you.

How did that affect you?

Reflect on a story when someone you love told you that you were broken in some way.

How did you handle it?

Chapter 5:

Calluses from Masks of Shame

Calluses are a thickening or hardening of the skin. This hardening happens by gripping things, tightly, or by punching things over and over again without protection. In sports, like martial arts, often this is executed as a discipline to develop thicker skin, a sort of iron fist. In music, particularly, playing the guitar requires toughening the fingertips. In breastfeeding, doctors encourage expectant mothers to "rough" their nipples in preparation. There is a purpose, and that purpose, oddly enough, is a means of protection. As you have probably already surmised, a similar hardening also occurs when we find ourselves developing a type of thick skin caused by shame. We develop a thick skin or iron fist from the gripping, strumming, and roughing that occurs in our minds daily. Shame clues us into situations that we desire to avoid. These calluses we develop over time can become so hardened that it is difficult to get to the initial cause of the wound over which these calluses developed. This coping process creates our "fig leaf" coverings. We use those fig leaves to create masks. These calluses may cause us to appear tough on the outside, but on the inside underlying infections from blisters developing is moving about your character that never properly healed. It grows, spreads, and affects other areas like cancer. Some use sarcasm as fig leaves to hide a deficiency in character. Some buckle down and apply a rigorous discipline to avoid the failure that seems imminent.

That was the way I dealt with my shame. As a matter of fact, it is one of the reasons I did not know I was living with hyperthyroidism. According to the Mayo clinic, hyperthyroidism happens when the thyroid gland makes too much thyroid hormone. This condition also is called overactive thyroid or Graves disease. Hyperthyroidism speeds up the body's metabolism. That can cause many symptoms, such as weight loss, hand tremors, and rapid or irregular heartbeat. I went undiagnosed for so long because of my work ethic and discipline. Hard work was how I dealt with life. I began losing weight and physical strength. I thought that I needed to work out harder and longer. It never dawned on me that I could be sick. I went to visit my Endocrinologist, she was blown away. She asked me how long had I been in this state? I had no answer for her. I truly did not know how long. I had been trying to cover up my physical deficiencies because I thought I was okay. I had learned to make weaknesses my strengths. I figured everything would work itself out. But, I wasn't okay. I was sick, not only sick, but closer to death than I or anyone else could have guessed. My fig leaves were thick and covered me pretty well; so much so, that I couldn't see myself. While some cope like me, others share embellished stories of life to hide the true shame underneath their calluses. In my journey, calluses began to develop because there was a short-sighted self-awareness. As I said earlier, shame's foundation is the idea that something is frighteningly wrong with me. I don't measure up.

I was an honor roll student most of my life. I graduated from Old Dominion University's school of Engineering. My undergrad degree is a Bachelor of Science in Electrical Engineering Technology (shout out to ODU class of 95). I never thought that I was really smart or intellectually gifted. It wasn't until I began taking IQ tests and heard others (people I considered intelligent) comment that I was intelligent that I began to believe it for myself. Unfortunately, because I didn't believe it, I thought I had to do everything in my power to keep up this perception. After all, if I am bright, everyone should know it. I made that standard up and embraced it as an expectation for me. Shame told me that if everyone doesn't know then perhaps it is not true. If I am inferior, the obvious solution is to remove the weakness or defer it to focus on some desired strength. In the words of Ultron, the marvel nemesis of Ironman, "humanity is weak and incapable of doing what is necessary." I think in some ways I want to be like Iron man. I want to place myself inside an armored suit where I can not be touched with the pain of being gripped, strummed, or "roughed". I would be impervious, but not invisible, that would be horrible. I would appear powerful. I would be something more and not something less. Do you resonate with this desire for super power? Yet, this is the opposite of why superheroes wear a mask. According to Stan Lee's comics the hero wears a mask to protect his/her loved ones. Not in this case, we create masks and wear them for protection of ourselves. Perhaps you could say we are protecting our shameful identity. It is not because we have a hidden strength or super power, but we do so to hide a prominent weakness. We have been convinced by our shame that this weakness is the reason why we don't experience true love. In order to address these calluses and heal the blisters, wounds, bruises, and infections underneath, we must first understand what caused us to develop them. We must get to the root causes. Sure, we know the calluses were formed by repetitively gripping tightly, but we must revisit what we were gripping to, when, how often, for how long and why so tightly. There are many different masks people wear to hide their shame. The time would fail us to try and name every fig leaf we use to craft masks. Okay these are two of my favorites: there is the mask of perfectionism. Oh and this next one might sound familiar, the mask of people-pleasing. There is even a mask of self-sabotage. Have you ever heard someone say, "I am in my own way?" Do you ever see them getting out of their own way so that they might be able to thrive. We all know people who wrestle with shame from their past due to poor personal decisions and circumstances out of their control. We have interacted with that person that never has anything right to wear to an event or for some reason just can't make it. They want to be there for you but it just has to be perfect and nothing is good enough. In fact, sometimes those same people will beg to be included, but often turn down invites. Ultimately they do not want anyone to view them from their past. Why even think that someone would? Before long, their complaint is a self-fulfilling prophecy. They claim no one invites them to anything, and no one does anymore because people get tired of being stood up. It could all change with the removal of the mask. Several of us have on more than one mask. Now the real work begins, but we have to have the courage to cross those raging waters embellished by shame.

REFLECTION:

What masks might you be wearing as a result of shame?

What are some of the calluses that have developed in your life due to coping with shame?

Reflect on a time when you were hurt or embarrassed, how did you cope with the situation?

Name some other masks that people might wear.

Chapter 6:

Crossing the Oceans - Empowered by Shame

Let's talk about the metaphorical journey of walking on top of the oceans of shame. As we move forward you may want to get your life jacket. Applying the information that comes next will help you, but you must take responsibility. With great powers comes great responsibility. I encourage you to apply self-compassion and self-forgiveness, and in the times you fall short of that, to remember that this is a journey. I want to share practical tools and exercises for navigating the emotional waters of shame and building resilience, but I also want to warn you about the strength of these waters. Let's not get it twisted! Don't think shame does not come with its own power. As we have discussed, shame comes with its own power and clothing line. That is correct, shame can actually empower you. Some of the things that have happened to us, embarrassed us and caused a tremendous amount of humiliation can make us appear strong. As a result, we emerge from some of those failures with power. I remember watching movies and cartoons growing up. I enjoyed acting out what I saw on the screen. One time when I was acting out what I had seen, I was having my way with my opponent. My opponent was bigger and stronger than I. It wasn't long before he was not happy about the interaction. He tackled me to the ground and began to wail on me. My motion picture went very bad. It was nothing like the movie and it never really is. Suddenly my hero came outside to rescue me. My hero did not have a cape and cowl but was dressed in a skirt and apron. It was my mom who came to my rescue. I remember feeling so embarrassed that I had to be rescued at all, but what is worse is that I had to be rescued by my mom. I wasn't even able to take care of myself. I promised myself I would never again need to be rescued. Maybe you have had a similar thought after a specific event. 'I'll never be hurt like that again!'

That moment of over compensation and dependence on myself did make me feel powerful, but as you can imagine, I was soaking in shame. This shame provided a relentless motivation in me to become a defender of the weak. I would be the hero and not the victim. I was really projecting and fighting for my own self-worth, when the main person degrading me was me. Who told me I was without help or strength? My ego did. I was motivated. A new and tremendous opportunity opened up in my life to workout and study all sorts and kinds of fighting styles and martial arts that equipped and made me courageous. It is the same false sense of power that would bring me to a place where most who encountered me would feel like I was unapproachable. It seemed like it took me forever, I mean a very long time, almost 30 years to figure out why I appeared to be so unapproachable to others. In my opinion, I was humble, willing, open and lovable. Why wouldn't they see me as a defender of the weak? But several people said they felt the exact opposite. It's kind of like trying to hug a porcupine or a cactus, but yet I had no idea that the instance of shame had created prickly fig leaves. Shame had actually created that armor I mentioned earlier and I didn't even know. I guess at some level, I was Iron man, but not in a good way. Shame is a master in creating hiding places to mask the truth. As introduced earlier, shame also creates a new identity where you could end up with an alter ego. I think that's why a lot of us like comics and action movies. We like heroes and villains. I think they provide an escape where we can vicariously engage our own trauma without actually having to think about our personal experiences. We tell ourselves it is okay to wear a mask. We have to wear it. While in a culture where our new heroes don't mind taking off the mask, many are unaware that the first one we shed is often only the first layer. We don't care if people know who we are. The problem is we are unable, at times, to recognize that the mask is in layers. We're unable to get behind the shame that created the shame. Upon this discovery, we can begin to sail into the waters of our unmasked shame where an opportunity to step out of the boat awaits. The problem is that shame has been working like a well-oiled machine, sometimes for decades. While we can be empowered by shame, we also have the opportunity to unmask the shame, deal with the root issue and begin to reroute that power for our healing. The journey will be tough, especially if you believe you can't swim and drowning is imminent. You may find out that you do not want to deal with the shame. The shame can create a sense of pride that says, "It's too deep, too much, and too late for me." We sound like Darth Vader in his words to Luke in Return of the Jedi. Ian Kron, author of the book the Road Back to You, often says, "we create narratives and coping mechanisms that help us navigate life, but often those same narratives and coping mechanisms keep us from experiencing what we really want." We are left with a decision. Attack it or allow it to continue to attack us. Sink or swim.

REFLECTION:

What does freedom look like for you?

How do you know when you are living as your free, full self?

What masks in your life have made you appear to be strong?

How would you finish the question, 'Who told you that you were _____?'

Chapter 7:

Liberation through Vulnerability

Let's talk about trust and vulnerability. Our ability to appropriately and thoroughly address shame depends upon our ability to open up, even to our own selves. Professor Brené Brown is a renowned author and podcast host. She is known for her work on shame and trust through vulnerability. She defines trust as risking and making something precious to me vulnerable to the actions of others. Often, especially when engaging in this kind of work, a quick cost-benefit analysis concludes that the rewards of vulnerability do not outweigh the risk of being vulnerable. Vulnerable comes from a word that means "wounded." Because of this notion of potential hurt, we often treat trust in relationships like money. When our trust account is low, vulnerability is not worth the cost for our relational net worth. We are not as willing to risk the expense of vulnerability. The cost of building new relationships (and sometimes sustaining old ones) can affect our relational portfolio, so we believe we are lacking the relational capital to take the risk. This is problematic because God made us for relationships. Building relationships must become a priority because it is such a necessary part of our growth. Even when the ratio I have to pay is higher than my desire to pay the cost, the truth is the rewards far outweigh the risk. I can exponentially and infinitely build my relational capital. Still, shame will tell us the risk is too great, we are in danger. I believe vulnerability is taking something very near and dear to me and trusting you with its exposure. There is power in vulnerability. Building relationships with vulnerability as a priority can be used as a means to exposing shame and become the catalyst for healing that leads to transformation. This opportunity must be explored. Together, we can tap into this power. Have you ever felt like you mastered something, but you really didn't? Have you ever felt the surge of confidence from knowing that you can accomplish a task without thinking because you have spent so much time solving a problem, only to find the issue recurs and the solutions vary. Maybe you had the thought, " I finally figured out what my problem is and I will never let that happen to me again." Only to find out that very thing that's always been an issue, always been a problem is right there still haunting you. You quickly learned it still plagues and eats at you. This feeling is kind of like a papercut. Have you ever cut your finger on a piece of paper? If so, you know what it's like when you have a paper cut and you reach in your pocket for your keys or wallet, and you just wish your whole finger was missing. That is slightly exaggerated for emphasis, however this nagging pain is accompanied with exaggeration. This paper cut experience is a similar experience to covered shame. Covered shame will continue to bother us like a jammed finger injury. Like any nagging injury, it not only affects us, but it affects us at the best of times and the worst of times. There have been so many times when I thought I had victory over my shame. I did the hard work of sharing my story and I thought that was enough. I was with an intimate group of people. We begin confessing sins, failures, and shortcomings. I began sharing my brokenness openly for the very first time. I not only shared stories of my shame, but also why the stories came about. I shared how the initial traumatic event placed me on Shame Avenue heading South. I left that group empowered by the blessing of confession. After shedding a few tears, which I rarely did, I put on my signal light and turned right onto Victory Highway heading North. I thought I had discovered what was holding me back. Now I'm ready to be the best version of myself or so I thought. We want to become the best version of ourselves; but often we'll be let down. I was disappointed because I didn't know that

I didn't deal with the root of my shame. Remember the traumatic event and sharing of it does not align with what happened inside of you when the event occurred. The traumatic events can be shared in detail as facts, but that does not equal what was experienced in the heart. We often share instances of shame and believe that we're okay. But, we must address the reason why we began to hide in the first place by asking the questions, "What made me feel the need to be covered? What made me feel naked in the first place?" Maybe you were molested or knew someone was being mistreated and you felt helpless to do anything about it. Maybe you stole something from someone that you knew had given so much to you. Maybe you made a poor decision that you regretted immediately because it not only affected your life, but your parents or siblings or children. Maybe you said words to someone you truly love in front of others who thought you would never do that, but the words came out in a raging moment of anger. You still can't believe you let those words out of your mouth. Perhaps those instances embarrassed you in such a way that you felt the need to hide. But you still feel that "paper cut" every day and the wound is growing, and the pain won't subside, no matter how you try to medicate it.

For example, if someone has been molested or abused they forget to admit that they could have enjoyed a part of what happened before they recognized that they have been manipulated, tampered with and wounded. In other words, It's possible that a person may feel shame because they believe they allowed themselves to be mistreated. A person may blame him or herself, or maybe even feel guilty that there was any pleasure in something that was "so wrong." The discovery is because they've hidden the fact that the true reason for the shame has been absorbed in a coping strategy often unbeknownst to them. We disregard the feelings and do our best to act like they are not true or never existed. The angry words that came out might have truly been how a person felt at the time, but overall, the words weren't true. Shame tells us we never should have felt that way, thus making the lashing out even worse. If you resonate or become enraged because of the scenarios I just mentioned, please understand that I am sharing with you from my own experience stories that I have heard or been a major role player. I too know this paper cut feeling. I would be lying to you if I said none of the punches I threw felt good. I hurt people and at times, didn't even care. It's shameful, but what made me want to hide is at times, I felt good about it. I felt powerful. I felt like a hero. But I wasn't. So yes, I know that nagging pain, and unless we do something drastic about it, we may never want to be free. I may have shared my instance of trauma with others, but I had never truly dealt with the reason I felt shame, and there could have been a lot of different reasons. I had to really try to figure out what was happening inside of me during the instance of pain caused by some traumatic events. Just to be transparent, another issue that surfaced is there had been many other instances added to my narrative since then, making it extremely difficult to get to a place where I could really pinpoint the true reason for my shame. I have discovered that many of us also have selective amnesia as it relates to this topic of vulnerability. We often can not really remember what happened. Sometimes this is true. Other times it is not true. When that is the case you will find that even though you dealt with instances of shame you'll be let down again. There are ways to access those memories that feel locked. This lurking feeling of lack of closure and being let down again has the potential to strangle the life out of you and lead you to a true catastrophe. You must desire to do the hard work of peeling back the layers of fig leaves. So how do we do it? I want to provide some guidance on how we cultivate vulnerability in relationships and create an environment of acceptance. Keep these three concepts in mind:

(1) Communicate openly about your emotions.
(2) Show empathy and use active listening skills.
(3) Share personal experiences to foster trust.

Communicate openly and honestly about your emotions and share how you feel. Perhaps in the past you have sought to please others, and that kept you from acknowledging how you truly felt. The more we are concerned with the person we may disappoint, the less likely we will be completely honest. Be more concerned with your health than their disappointment. These moments are about you loving yourself. When we openly and honestly acknowledge how we feel, we can truly hear ourselves. Sometimes I may not know what I really think or how I really feel about something until I say it out loud. There is something both jarring and freeing about hearing ourselves speak up. So often we cope in isolation and keep these feelings bottled up, thinking they may be destructive. Sometimes we don't believe we will have a listening ear. Who really cares anyway, right? That's what shame says. When you are being vulnerable you must share how you feel in a raw and uncut way. You are speaking to be understood. Now that does not mean uncensored, where anything goes to anyone and everyone, anywhere, and every time. It means we learn to show up as our most authentic self and refuse to be silenced by others, including our shame.

Secondly, you must show empathy and use active listening skills. Often when you share in such a vulnerable way, there will be a response. We must be willing to hear the response. We need to listen carefully. We are not listening for judgment or condemnation. We are listening for clarity. The response comes in forms of tone of speech, body language and actual words. We are listening to know whether or not I communicated in such a way that others could understand what was being shared. Keep in mind, the person listening may be hearing this information for the first time, so we must also be sensitive to their experience, and aware of how our actions may affect them.

Thirdly, Share personal experiences to foster trust.

Trust must be built. There must be a shared understanding. Common bonds are developed through telling real stories about our lives because we are real people. Trust is necessary for our relational survival. Trust me, shame will whisper in your ear, urging that there is no one you can trust. Shame will bring up every time there has been hurt or anytime trust has been broken. Shame is embellishing the opportunity so that it may protect itself. There are stories of individuals who have embraced vulnerability and experienced profound personal growth.

We all, at different times and with varying degrees of intensity, must press through the lies and seek other foresters who know the fig leaves well enough to identify them. I call this person a wingman. It's like a pilot that has a wingman. The term wingman most likely originated in aviation communities before the arrival of fighter jets. A wingman was used in combat aviation. Pilots flying in formation refer to the pilot immediately next to them, usually on their right as their "wingman." The "wingman" was the man on their wing. This is precisely what we need in life. Each of us should have people on either side of us helping us in the fight for emotional health and self awareness. The war wages on and battles ensue; but, soon the war subsides and is won through trust and vulnerability. It is okay to cry out, someone please help me! Seek out friends or relatives that you can exercise these three concepts with to practice vulnerability.

REFLECTION:

What are specific instances you remember feeling shame?

If you were to create a personal trust chart like an organizational flow chart, how would it look?

Begin with who you trust most and go from there. Put individuals or groups of individuals you trust on the same lines.

As you review your chart, why do you trust them?

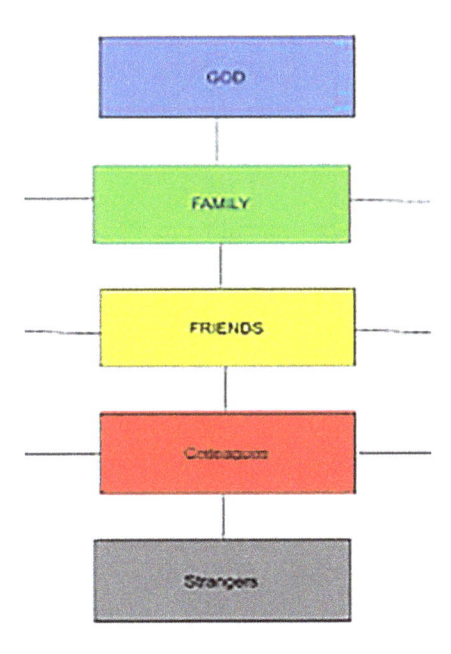

```
┌──────────────┐
│     GOD      │
└──────┬───────┘
       │
┌──────┴───────┐
│    FAMILY    │
└──────┬───────┘
       │
┌──────┴───────┐
│   FRIENDS    │
└──────┬───────┘
       │
┌──────┴───────┐
│  Colleagues  │
└──────┬───────┘
       │
┌──────┴───────┐
│   Strangers  │
└──────────────┘
```

Chapter 8:

Shame & Short Circuits

I wish we could travel back in time and review all the details of life. Ironically, shame often acts like a time machine taking us back to a feeling of embarrassment, a moment where we were the laughing stock of all our acquaintances. The ones that mattered most to us anyway. Whether they knew we existed wasn't the point at all. In these moments we may feel vulnerable, weak and unworthy. This feeling is indelibly forged in our mind. It is etched in our heads by memory recall and tattooed on the lintel of our hearts. A flood of memories takes us back to the feeling of that moment/event but without all of the details. The body still remembers as well, often reacting to what feels similar before the consciousness of our thoughts. A flashback becomes a flash flood with no boundaries or warnings. We instantaneously feel alone, weak, disturbed, or hopeless. Interestingly enough, if we stay there we will be alone with all the lies and embellishments told by an inner critic that sees you as the tragic hero of the story. In this narrative, oddly enough, our fate is perceived as what we deserve or worse than what we deserve. What should we do when we arrive at this point? Great question! I am glad you asked. Now it is time to seek a solution. We have to be brave. Shame short circuits so much of the life of its prey. A short circuit occurs when instead of the current flowing through an intended circuit path, something causes the flow of electricity to follow a different shorter path. Short circuits occur when a low-resistance path not suited to carry electricity receives a high-volume electrical current. Short circuits happen when a hot wire touches a conductive object it's not supposed to be touching. The result often damages the electronic device, making it slower than normal, faster than normal, delayed, or glitches. It could cause electrical shock, or could even start an electrical fire. This is analogous to the emotional experience that happens. You may have already connected how our lives are similarly affected when we are short circuited by shame. Let's view our life narrative and character as a series circuit. There is a linear trajectory that we are following. We grow from infant to toddler to child to teen to adolescent to young adult. Sometimes, before we develop into a fully functioning emotionally healthy adult, an event(s) occurs that impacts the series of development in a negative way. At that point, the way we see life itself begins to change. The flow of emotional energy jumps over certain stages of development and creates its own path to a shorter, more comfortable pathway. Sure, things seem to still function until this new pathway creates a glitch in your character. The glitch shocks at times and starts a fire at others. Little by little, we are ruining our spiritual, emotional, physical and/or social "electronics." Our connections are all adversely affected, as shame hijacks our personal coherent narratives. Your coherent narrative is life as it has realistically happened to you without embellishments. This new life with layers of fig leaves that create morphing masks is not the life we were supposed to live. But we do our best each day to cover the shame and embarrassment of feeling naked everywhere we go. My wife was a stay at home mom in the early 2000's and developed her own child care business. She watched many of the children of our friends and church members. Recently, I saw one of the young ladies all grown up. Unfortunately, I could hardly recognize her. My wife noticed her and asked her what her name was. The name she gave us was not the name given to her at birth and it certainly was not the name that we affectionately called her when she spent time in our home each day. But after asking a few more questions we figured out that this was the same girl that my wife had watched and protected when she was a toddler. She looked at me with a sullen smile and said "Yep, I am trash" Her words pierced me instantly and made me want to cry. Grab a tissue, it might have a similar effect on you. I immediately retorted, "What did you say?" She said it again. "I am trash." I mustered up all of the emotional strength I had in that moment and said, you are valuable, you are loved. You are not the sum total of your choices, mistakes or failures. Never say that again. You are not trash. I knew that feeling all too well though and maybe I'm not the only one. Have you ever felt like trash? Have you ever felt like Forky in Toy Story 4? Have you ever felt like giving up? That is the end of the road on Shame Avenue. This is the place that our shame and guilt can bring us to. The house is now on fire. Fire is blazing and the shock is so real that we sit right in the middle of the fire immobilized by the fear of the struggle to be free. Though we know that we are in danger, we are reluctant to move or cry out. Shame whispers, who would understand? Who would care? Who can you trust? No one will hear you if you scream. There is rescue from this burning building. Help is on the way. Healing is possible, but we must be brave. This is the time we begin to seek a solution.

REFLECTION:

What are some of the ways you describe yourself, positive or negative? Why?

What is the worst choice that you have ever made? What would you do differently if you could travel back in time?

What is the best choice that you have ever made? Why?

Take time to stare at yourself in a mirror for 3 minutes. Write down every thought you have during this time. Spend time reflecting on what thoughts you had, why you had them, where they came from, and how long they have been there.

Chapter 9:

Haunted by False Humility

Every step of the way from here on out, we must be careful. The first step in this process of healing and walking on the oceans of our shame is to humble ourselves. I have experienced that shame can deceive and provide a false humility that will circumvent or short circuit the healing process as well. There are times we believe we're acting out of humility but are really reacting out of a reverse sense of pride. This is what I mean by false humility. You see, pride says I must protect myself at all times. Humility says I must lower myself and value others as I value myself. False humility says in order to protect myself at all times I must be aware of every danger. For example, I may appear to place myself under others so that others might be able to accept me. After all, I need them to give me their approval and validation. Notice the purpose of my humbling is not to heal. It is not to face the truth. No, it is to receive what I am missing. It is again a mask to cope. Shame takes this appearance of humility and makes us believe that we are doing the right things for the right reasons when actually we are doing the right things for the wrong reasons. Sometimes we're doing the wrong things for the wrong reasons. For example, because of my past and dealing with substance abuse I decided not to drink any alcoholic beverages. When I go to a wedding or some event where drinking is encouraged, someone would ask me if I wanted a glass of wine for example. The Bible does not teach that drinking a glass of wine is wrong. It teaches me that it is unwise. The Bible teaches that being drunk is prohibited (see Ephesians 5:18). I would be convicted by my conscience and plead humility and say I could not drink and dishonor God. But in actuality, I had made a decision that I was unwilling to change. The decision was the right thing to do but it was made because of the shame created by substance abuse not because of my love for God. This then was the right action but it was made by the wrong reasoning. The right action in my case was to stop drinking. I personally did not find drinking to be wise. It was not something I desired to do and it had been a vice previously. The right thing to do is say I no longer drink alcohol. I will no longer allow alcohol to become a substance that I abuse. Then, when it made sense, like in the case of a wedding, I would be able to make a toast with a glass of Champagne with a clear conscience because it was not sin against God to do so. I now had a choice. I now regained my freedom. I was in bondage in both cases. On the one hand I had been an abuser of alcohol, on the other hand, I had become judgmental on the account of my discipline. Had I become more holy than the God I served? Or, was my way higher than His way and His way lower than mine? In the words of apostle Paul, Certainly not! This way of living was blasphemous. I was ignorant to this short circuit that was happening because the current appeared to still be flowing in the right direction. Positive outcomes were occurring in my life. This had to be right. It felt right. This must be the way, right? Wrong! Perhaps the most unfair thing is doing something the wrong way and having a positive outcome. This is what happens when false humility sneaks up behind you and steals your identity. You can begin to feel like your righteousness exceeds the righteousness of those around you. But this righteousness is your own making which does not lead to any type of freedom, it only leads to despair and you guessed it more shame. Israel had done the same thing, as Paul reminds them.

For they, being ignorant of God's righteousness, and seeking to establish their own righteousness, have not submitted to the righteousness of God. (Romans 10:3)

You begin to discourage others into thinking that they have to take the same road that you take and believe the same ideas that you believe in order to be right with God, when really it is your eyes that you are trying to please. You begin to look down on other people because they decide to drink even after they have come to have a relationship with God. You begin to encourage them through coercing them that this vice is something they need to give up all together. This coercion is not out of care and concern, it is out of judgment and manipulation. This is an example of telling someone to do the right thing for the wrong reason. Your motive is also wrong but you don't see it that way. Care for the individual you are influencing is not your concern. You want uniformity to your will. This is false humility at work. I was caught in this very plight. Drowning and being ignorant to the consequences of legalism and judgementalism. True humility would consider others and lead them to the truth. It is the truth that will set them free. It is the truth that has set me free. It is the truth that can set you free. Under the true essence of humility my life is laid vulnerable and bare for others to see as an example of what happens when we embrace our failure and victoriously walk on top of the oceans of our shame. There's no condemnation and there's no manipulation. People don't have to conform to me in order for me to accept them. I treat people as I want to be treated. I accept them just as they are. I love them enough to encourage them to be free. I desire to let people know what happened to me and how I have been set free. The actions we have taken to better ourselves should be shared. By now you probably have guessed that this type of behavior led by false humility will always result in a deeper sense of shame. You will never overcome shame by overcompensating with discipline.

You must deal with the root cause of your shame. Only after confronting the root cause will you be able to operate in true humility which is beautiful and full of courage.

REFLECTION:

In what ways have you seen false humility working in your life?

In your life experience, what are some examples of doing the right thing for the wrong reason?

What is your definition of humility?

Who would you consider to be a humble person? Why?

Chapter 10:

Family Call - Who Told Me I Was Naked?

My family has been trying to draw closer together. We all need to investigate our narratives from our beginnings and upbringings. I am the eldest of five children born to two wonderful parents. I made a public confession of my faith and confessed Jesus as my Savior at the age of 4. Despite the clear working of God in my life, I was angry. Several things happened in my life for which I was ashamed. You could probably name something and I would say that I was involved in it one way or another. My embarrassment ranged from sexual immorality, to the selling and abuse of drugs to violence. I rededicated my life to the Lord after being in a horrible car accident on the day of my college graduation. In 1995 my son was born to the young lady that I was dating. That lady is now my wife because of the grace and mercy of God in my life. After rededicating my life to Jesus, my life was different. I served God and witnessed much of His life changing power. I answered the call to proclaim God's Word in 1998. I was licensed to preach in October 2000. I knew my purpose was to passionately unmask the deception of Satan and self. My love for Jesus motivated me to proclaim God's truth. My mission verse is

> "For <u>I am not ashamed</u> of the gospel of Christ it is the power of God unto salvation to everyone who believeth to the Jew first and also to the Greek." (Romans 1:16).

Did you see in the verse above, I am not ashamed? Well, I wasn't ashamed of the gospel. However, it was through a series of family calls that I began to understand that something inside of me was still in need of repair. In order to get to the root of shame it may require you to do some difficult work with your family of origin. Sometimes the people that are closest to us and the people that we love the most, are the hardest people to get to listen to us. We need their listening ear. It is a great possibility that some of the instances of shame came from those very same people or from the absence of some of those people. There are so many circumstances that occur in life and within the family structure that can create the difficulties that lead to shame. It could be the death of a parent or sibling. It could be an alcoholic father or mother or, it could be a workaholic mother or father. It could be bad parenting. Either way someone ends up suffering. We have all experienced some level of dysfunction in our families. We have all experienced some level of brokenness. The Scripture says in Romans 3:23,

All have sinned and fall short of the glory of God.

This means there is no one that is perfect. There are no perfect parents. In my life and your life there are some failures and trauma. Also, the way we process life initially is going to be tainted with imperfection.

New Year's Eve

My life had been radically transformed by God. I was in my late twenties. I wanted to share this awakening with my family that as a result of my sin I had been estranged from for two years. Like the prodigal, I decided to return home. When God sent me home, I decided to deal with the shame that had kept me from my immediate family. I did not understand what I am trying to convey to you now. Therefore, I was only dealing with the instances of shame from the past and not with the root cause of the shame that had imposed its will in my life. I thought I was actually going to be able to deal with the root causes of my shame. I went home to celebrate Christmas and it was right around New Year's Eve. At that point in time, I thought the cause of my shame was my disobedience to God and my parents. I lived a prodigal life with drugs and alcohol. I was violent. I was always angry. This was until God captured my heart in the car accident that changed my entire life. The lady I was dating, who is now my wife, ended up pregnant. I was the father. I grew up in a loving home. I knew right from wrong. I chose to do what was wrong. I chose to deal with the consequences of my wrong. How long would I be punished? It was time to deal with this shame. Therefore, I went on sharing with my family shameful things that I had done in my past. I invited my family also to share if there were things that they had done that no one around our table knew about but wanted to share and be set free. Yes, free! Free? I thought this would be the moment that we all had been waiting for in life. I thought this was the moment that I would be free and be able to walk in a powerful way in my life with the support of my family. What happened next is the thing that postponed my freedom for the next 20 years. A family member whom I love and trust communicated to me that I was experiencing a level of pride. He said that I thought I was better or more spiritual than the people in my family. At that moment I really felt this person was correct. I had a high regard for the opinion of this individual. I felt like he was right and I was wrong. I reasoned that pride had grabbed me again, taking my place impersonating me and speaking for me. I was let down, but still confident because my life had changed and that could not be mistaken or denied. Another instance of shame led to a deeper shame couched in false humility. Perhaps something like this has happened to you. When we are on our road to self awareness and emotional health, we find deceptive and temporary respites along the way. It's kinda like the common cold, we believe we've found the cure to a disease. It lies dormant in our body waiting for the right moment to strike. We are not totally rid of it.

I just have to work harder. I never once thought about the question "Who told you, you were naked?" In my case, who told you you were prideful? This person was my father. My dad was my inspiration. He was and still is the most consistent person I have ever met. I lived with him. I had never seen him sin. I knew he was not perfect but there was nothing that I could point to in his life and believe that he was not trustworthy. His opinion mattered. He is a godly man. He never says things just to say something. He says what he sees. And what he sees is true, or so I thought at the time. Was that the truth at that moment? I never gave it a second thought. I found out I was still broken. I thought I found the answer to my problems. I thought I'd go and face it with my brand new spiritual superpowers. So much for those powers. What kind of power leaves you deceived by hidden shame? Shame was still hidden for the next twenty years of my life. I was better but I was not totally free. I was walking on water but still sinking. I was used by God to do some extraordinary things to communicate the message of the cross of Jesus with passion. I have been privileged by God's grace to see many people, particularly young people, come to faith in Jesus and have an understanding of what it means to be His disciple. I continued to grow and work hard with hidden shame for twenty years. Within this twenty year time period, I was called to pastor a church. Imagine, here I am about to pastor Jesus' bride, which I'm absolutely excited about and believe I'm equipped for, with shame embedded deep within my soul. I was soaring but boxed in by boundaries constructed by shame. I was free within a prison. This shame kept me from being the husband, father and pastor that God was calling me to become. There was always self doubt and a desire to please people through performance. All you had to do was mention that I was operating in pride or that I thought I was always right for me to immediately shrink back into false humility and ignore the issue at hand. Or worse, allow bad decisions to move forward. My leadership was impacted by shame. The day came that changed everything for real and for good. I had been praying for a year for God to help me love recklessly and lead courageously. God answered my prayer.

The call

Twenty years later I was speaking with another one of my brothers. We were speaking of so many things that have shaped us. He has a youtube channel called "your next cast." If you are enjoying this story of my life please check out his channel and subscribe. Place this book title in the comments #Who Told you you were NAKED. Thank you in advance for your support of his channel. It was this brother who said that what I was told twenty years earlier was not true. I had never heard these words spoken to me. Never had I questioned the words. Never had I thought what if the words were not true. He continued to say that I should not have been told what I was told. Instead perhaps the people that I had put so much trust in really had let me down. Wait, are you saying I should question authority in my life? Question the one figure I trusted the most? The Spirit was leaping for joy and tugging on my heart like a toddler at the ice cream parlor saying to me listen and make the jump! At that very moment, I was gripped with a feeling that is hard to describe. It was a feeling of excitement and a feeling of deep sorrow. Yet a feeling of expectancy and joy as well. It was a feeling from a vision of freedom! It was a feeling of power! In that very moment as tears began to flow I began to understand what had happened. I had not rightly accessed my shame. I had not operated in total truth. No wonder I was not absolutely free. I had made my parents an idol. Specifically I had subliminally made my dad an idol.

Therefore, in my eyes, he could do no wrong. It was through a series of events that God opened my eyes to see things that made this life changing encounter possible. I heard God whisper in my heart, I did not tell you that you were naked. I told you that you are loved! I told you that you are mine!

REFLECTION:

What ways can you identify with this story?

Who might you need to have a conversation with today?

Write down some of the feelings you have right now?

Chapter 11:

The Fight: The Answer to the Question

We must understand that our fight is not a human fight, it is a spiritual fight. It is a war. We are not fighting against flesh and blood but against an adversary who knows us all too well.

> *For we do not wrestle against flesh and blood, but against principalities, against powers, against the rulers of the darkness of this age, against spiritual hosts of wickedness in the heavenly places. (Ephesians 6:12)*

This enemy is the one who set up our fore parents in the beginning. He told Eve that she was missing something. Satan, the serpent of old, told her that she could be like God because the tree had power and privilege that God was keeping from her. After being deceived, she disobeyed. She also gave to Adam her husband and he disobeyed. After this disobedience, there was a preoccupation with self and comparison which led to the discovery that they were naked. Designer clothing, Fig leaves of Eden, was created.

> *Then the eyes of both of them were opened, and they knew that they were naked; and they sewed fig leaves together and made themselves coverings. (Genesis 3:7)*

Shame showed them that they were naked, then they told themselves that they were naked.

God asked them after they had disobeyed Him.

"Who told you that you were naked? Have you eaten from the tree of which I commanded you that you should not eat?" (Genesis 3:11)

Before the disobedience they were naked. Nothing had changed with them physically on the outside but everything changed mentally, emotionally and spiritually on the inside. They were now disconnected from God. This caused them to view each other based on physical appearance and self estimation. God asked a question and presented an answer. The question: Who told you you were naked? The answer in the form of a question: have you eaten from the tree? Eating from the tree led to disappointment, empty promise and disconnection from God which is spiritual death. It led to pride, shame and also physical death.

This claim shame makes to us and about us is difficult to shake because the assertion comes from us and is validated by the world around us.

We must fight and seek help because we are blinded by the deceitfulness of sin. We need help to see our blind spots and hear our false assertions that become concrete over time. We tell ourselves things that may be true on one hand, but give us no reason to hide. The truth for Adam and Eve was that they were naked. But there was no need to cover up. Ultimately, shame is the great cover up. According to the Barna group (a christian research organization) 56% of Christians feel their spiritual life is entirely private?

A man who isolates himself seeks his own desire; He rages against all wise judgment. (Proverbs 18:1)

Pride has a strategy. The strategy is to isolate you. It is illusive and claims to be shy. Another detective is needed to help in solving the mystery. Shame has been covering our flaws and our mistakes so that we make excuses instead of taking responsibility. Are you naked? If that is the truth, how should you respond? Is your response to the instance or the idea of shame valid? Once you begin to address these things you are well on your way to deal with the shame and become empowered to be the best version of you. Shame breeds masking. Masks are worn by heroes and villains. We are always told in the action packed hero drama that the mask is used to protect the ones you love. Have you ever thought about why villains wear masks? Why would a bank robber wear a mask? "This is a stick up," comes to mind. When shame is birthed this is its exact sentiment. Shame causes us to surrender our rights to a ruthless bully. In order to protect myself, I put on a mask. This mask can be anything from what I want you to believe about me, to agreeing with the way you see me. The issue with this is that instead of taking this mask off after some social feat is achieved, I find myself putting on another mask to build a new character for the storyline I have augmented. I now believe that this is who I am or at least who I want to be. Neither is true. At this point, I really don't know who I am. The masks continue to stack and cover up. At some point if a person is not well polished and practiced the pain of holding it all together can lead to substance abuse. Ironically substance abuse hinges on the idea of masking the pain. Often this pain is created from masking shame. This in and of itself is a shame no pun intended. My sons went to public school in Prince George's county MD. They wanted to hide the fact that they had two loving parents at home. The schools were unbalanced with single parent families. They wanted their peers, at that time, to believe that they too were raised by wolves. This experience is very disheartening to say the least, but it illustrates my point that shame can lead to false identities.

A friend of mine shared with me that he lied to his friends about seeing his dad because his dad was not in his life. He wanted dad there badly so he could identify with his friends. He told them a believable story to hide the pain of shame. Shame cuts to the core of one of humanity's deepest needs. The need to be known. The Bible calls this in 1 John 2:16 the pride of life.

> *For all that is in the world—the lust of the flesh, the lust of the eyes, and the pride of life—is not of the Father but is of the world.*

Whatever we have that can make others believe we are famous highlights our desire to be known. Shame says that no one wants to know you because of this glaring point of physical look or psychological outlook. If you hide this thing, then no one will know and you will be known. This lie is problematic on at least two fronts. The first issue with this lie is that people who actually want to get to know you will see you with the mask. The second issue with this lie is that hiding does not promise that people will encounter something different and want to know you. In both cases the true self is not known. We still fall for this lie hook, line and sinker. To use another fishing analogy, I am convinced that soft bait plastics work. However, I have seen fish look at a lure and totally ignore it. That experience is pretty rare when you have live bait. Once fish notice the movement of the live bait they strike. You can catch a lot of fish with an artificial lure but if fish would rather have the real thing shouldn't we? We spend a lot of time manufacturing plastics for our personalities. The real thing with the right presentation will yield results every time. There is much more to say about "not being fake." When shame is involved, there is a great chance that you are not dealing with an authentic person. This person needs to understand who they are. They must fight to become the most authentic version of themselves. They must be empowered to break the chains of pride forged by the comfort of shame. You can do this too.

REFLECTION:

Name instances where you told yourself something that was not true?

Pinpoint areas in your life where shame has caused you to compare yourself to others?

Who told you that you were naked?

Chapter 12:

CAUTION: Willpower is Not Always on Will Call

SHAME can stop a leader from reaching his or her full potential. It can cause you to avoid necessary conflict. And it can make a person become passive where a much more direct approach is needed. Communication becomes convoluted. As a leader you are sometimes accused of the old fashioned way namely, it is my way or the highway. And really no servant leader wants to bear that burden. However, the burden for leadership is to provide clear direction for others. A leader has to make a decision in areas where responsibility is solely or at least primarily placed on their shoulders. Shame will cause a leader to defer. This could lead to a decision that creates difficulty for a family member or corporate unit. This lack of leadership could stem from a false sense of humility that developed from shame. The courage we need to lead in difficult times instead of using manipulation is often missing. Our willpower is not always on willcall. Empowerment means that if the same shame causing experiences were to come about again, I would now make different decisions. When we sense the urgency we must move forward with reckless abandon because our desire to do what is right is not always available. Let us proceed, but let us do so with extreme caution. We are about to move into the nuts and bolts of how to become free from shame. Shame will resist every step of the way. We must be resilient and steadfast. Here is our new acrostic to begin the journey to freedom.

The acrostic vs the acronym

Selflessness
Humility
Accountability
Mastery &
Endurance

Vs

Should
Have
Already
Mastered
Everything

Selflessness

The journey to true humility will require a selfless attitude. Selflessness is a preoccupied concern for the needs and wishes of others more than self. The Apostle Paul says in Philipians 2:3-4:

> *3 Let nothing be done through selfish ambition or conceit, but in lowliness of mind let each esteem others better than himself. 4 Let each of you look out not only for his own interests, but also for the interests of others.*

I have learned that what is needed is a healthy love for self or self care. In other words, look out for yourself but not only for yourself. Seek to understand the perspectives of others by looking through their lens, and standing in their shoes. Do this not at the expense of self but with the freest expression of self. That is impossible without humility. In fact, the practice of healthy self-care really begins with a true sense of humility.

Humility

The journey to true humility will require an attitude that embraces selfcare but is not selfish. The word humility comes from a Latin root and means "earth." It carries the idea of seeing ourselves "of earth." In other words, we see ourselves as mortals, created from dust in God's image with equal value and shared purpose. We can stack ourselves up against all other competitors, God included, and see the greatness of the equality of our smallness in comparison with God. When we see ourselves in this down to earth sense, we can place ourselves alongside others. Our equal value and shared purpose help us to see ourselves and others as equals, and therefore in need of treatment according to the way we each would desire to be treated. Seeing differences causes us to put value judgments on others, causing us to compare and esteem others on unjust scales that we have created. This view postures pride as viewing others at odds rather than as equals. But to see one another as with equal value and shared purpose allows us to esteem others better than ourselves. We become accountable to treat others with the inherent value with which we have been endowed by God, knowing that raising them up, does not mean putting ourselves down. What a freeing experience! We must then be held accountable for this practice of humility.

Accountability

Those closest to us will be able to help us with what we see and help us see what they see. That is one of the reasons relationship building is so important. We have blind spots. When we drive, often other vehicles enter the zone where the mirror can no longer display the image. For years, we had to turn our heads to see (and many of us still do); but, today's technology has sensors to help us with our blind spots. The people in our lives act as sensors.

They provide us with accountability. They keep us on the right path, reminding us of our humanity and equality. Accountability is the responsibility of providing an explanation for decisions and actions. It provides the opportunity to express what we want, how badly we want it, how we plan to get it, and how we will handle the adversity that comes along the way. Accountability then reflects on our responsibilities in light of our commitments, asking how much of our desired outcome have we received. Some of the things that we will begin to experience in accountability relationships are the very things that we have wanted all along. While we might have settled for the feelings of acceptance in the past, accountability says we are not on the journey to be accepted anymore. We are not working FOR approval. We are working FROM approval. We are on the journey to healing. Let us hold each other so close and so dear, that we hold one another accountable to the mastery of this type of God-honoring humility.

Mastery

My younger brother has a saying he uses often when training athletes, "Practice does not make perfect, Practice makes permanent." (Shout out to Timotheus Pope, CEO of Citizidz aka SB2DUB) Any action that we practice will become permanently resident in our psyche. This is how shame has operated in the background for so long. We practiced shame but did not know that we were practicing shame for years. As we practice true humility, we will begin to experience a level of mastery. Mastery is the end goal of all learning. Mastery is a comprehensive knowledge of a skill or subject, evidenced through the achievement of the maximum effect with the most efficiency and minimum effort. Mastery has an unconscious competence that can complete the task without directly thinking about it. The mastery of humility sounds a little like a paradox. How does one master humility when doing so inherently means not making oneself the focus? The objective here is to quickly realize when pride is at play and to know our own wishes and desires well enough to equally treat others the way we desire as a "second nature." Realizing pride aids and fosters the practice of vulnerable confession as well as promotes healing. Once we are able to master walking in humility then we must keep the practice consistent. Education is certainly a facet of mastery, but the sharpest distinction between proficiency and mastery is endurance.

Endurance

This is a process. It takes time. Just like mastering a subject in the academic arena through trial, test, practice and experience, so we learn humility. Surgeons have a mantra that helps them master their skill. "See one. Do one. Teach one." All throughout their careers, surgeons watch other master surgeons perform surgery, perform surgery themselves with masters watching, and teach others to perform surgeries. Their skills are not kept sharp by simply doing surgeries each day, even though that is what they do. They also keep their skills sharp by spending time with other masters and students swimming in their processes to reach unconscious competence. Whether surgeons, professional athletes, martial artists, mechanics, or other professions that seek to be masters of their craft, all who will be successful will spend countless hours conversing, watching film, practicing new techniques, sharpening old skills, taking on new challenges and refining processes. All the while, humility helps these sages of institutional knowledge operate with the continual mindset of a beginner. In doing so, endurance, while hard, never really feels like work. That is the way to freedom, and that road begins with serious self-care and true humility.

God knows we are limited in our expressions of love. He knows us very well. He knows us better than we know ourselves (see Psalm

139). It is God who asks the question who told you you were naked. Now it is time for you to answer the question. Who told you you lacked value? Who told you that you did not measure up? Who told you no one cares about you? Who told you depressing things that haunt you? What you will learn is whoever told you that is at best deceived and at worst a liar. Often the person who is to blame is the one looking back at us in the mirror. Yes, often the person who lied to us was us. The next time you look into a mirror I want you to tell yourself that you see another one of God's miracles looking back at you. God is the source of life, the savior of the lost in our world. God is the soul's true lover. Therefore, it is God who asks the question with your best interest in mind. Who told you that you were naked? In other words, who lied to you? You need to arm your mind with what God says about you

> *8 The LORD is merciful and gracious, Slow to anger, and abounding in mercy.*
>
> *9 He will not always strive with us, Nor will He keep His anger forever. 10 He has not dealt with us according to our sins, Nor punished us according to our iniquities. 11 For as the heavens are high above the earth, So great is His mercy toward those who fear Him; 12 As far as the east is from the west, So far has He removed our transgressions from us. 13 As a father pities his children, So the LORD pities those who fear Him. 14 For He knows our frame; He remembers that we are dust. 15 As for man, his days are like grass; As a flower of the field, so he flourishes. 16 For the wind passes over it, and it is gone, And its place remembers it no more. 17 But the mercy of the LORD is from everlasting to everlasting On those who fear Him, And His righteousness to children's children, 18 To such as keep His covenant, And to those who remember His commandments to do them. (Psalm 103:8-17)*

REFLECTION:

Which of the following words best describe your current state of mind: bitter or tender? angry or joyful? betrayed or beloved? critical or congratulatory? negative or positive? pessimistic or hopeful? resentful or content? Why?

Which part of the S.H.A.M.E acrostic do you need to begin with? Why?

What is something you can change right now that will empower you to become a more authentic version of yourself?

Chapter 13:

Shame Shame Go Away - Empty Your Cup

How do you protect yourself from shame? How do you face shame? Nothing can erase the impact of shame like confession. Confession is the key to release shame. Confession is to shame what forgiveness is to blame. These are great equalizers. They cancel each other out. This is why the Bible says to confess your faults to one another that you may be healed in James 5:16. Confession means to speak what is true. It is honesty about a situation. This honesty is communicated by the one that has the most to lose by the confession. I must say that this freedom leads to empowerment that is on another level. This is no longer survival. Once you confess the cause of shame and what happened inside of you during the event of trauma, then there is no way for shame to use its vice grip on your life in that particular area again. The pain may be there but the shame has nowhere to hide. Healing has begun. The song can be sung, Shame shame go away and come again another day. Only in this rendition of the nursery rhyme, it is truly rendered powerless. It will not be allowed to return. Confidence, strength and freedom are experienced in this expression leading to a new identity. Are you ready to be set free? People who are free of shame really do trust the Lord because this trust leads them to the humility needed to uncover and disarm shame. Trusting in God is the cure for shame.

Trust

My shame came from trusting in myself to compete and rise above my fears. This trusting in myself came from years of being let down by those I trusted. This means the only person who will not let us down is ourselves. Thus I trusted in myself. I wouldn't let myself down, or would I? But of course, I did. Time and time again, I let myself down. I failed myself. We must place our trust in God. He will not let us down. He never fails!

We must believe God's truth above every lie. Even if we are the ones found guilty of lying. The key is to learn from the Lord's love for us and His desire for us to thrive. This Psalm is written by someone who knows a great deal about shame and trusting God. Yes, this is the giant slayer but he also is a murderer and adulterer. Listen to King David the psalmist as he shows us how he dealt with shame.

> *1 To You, O LORD, I lift up my soul. 2 O my God, I trust in You; Let me not be <u>ashamed</u>; Let not my enemies triumph over me. 3 Indeed, let no one who waits on You be <u>ashamed</u>; Let those be <u>ashamed</u> who deal treacherously without cause. 4 Show me Your ways, O LORD; Teach me Your paths. 5 Lead me in Your truth and teach me, For You are the God of my salvation; On You I wait all the day. 6 Remember, O LORD, Your tender mercies and Your loving kindnesses, For they are from of old. 7 Do not remember the sins of my youth, nor my transgressions; According to Your mercy remember me, For Your goodness' sake, O LORD. 8 Good and upright is the LORD; Therefore He teaches sinners in the way. 9 The <u>humble</u> He guides in justice, And the <u>humble</u> He teaches His way. 10 All the paths of the LORD are mercy and truth, To such as keep His covenant and His testimonies. 11 For Your name's sake, O LORD, Pardon my iniquity, for it is great. 12 Who*

is the man that <u>fears</u> the LORD? Him shall He teach in the way He chooses. 13 He himself shall dwell in prosperity, And his descendants shall inherit the earth. 14 The secret of the LORD is with those who fear Him, And He will show them His covenant. 15 My eyes are ever toward the LORD, For He shall pluck my feet out of the net. 16 Turn Yourself to me, and have mercy on me, For I am desolate and afflicted. 17 The troubles of my heart have enlarged; Bring me out of my distresses! 18 Look on my affliction and my pain, And forgive all my sins. 19 Consider my enemies, for they are many; And they hate me with cruel hatred. 20 Keep my soul, and deliver me; **Let me not be ashamed, for I put my trust in You.** *21 Let integrity and uprightness preserve me, For I wait for You. 22 Redeem Israel, O God, Out of all their troubles! (Psalm 25)*

Trust in the Lord with all your heart and lean not to your own understanding (Proverbs 3:5) This may be the toughest yet most rewarding effort for us. Why is it so hard to trust God? Is it because we can't see Him? Or is it because we can't see Him at work in our lives? Do we believe we truly have a better plan? Our joy is incomplete where shame exists. Trusting the Lord brings a joy and a peace that is not able to be measured. It never runs out. Imagine being free from shame forever. It is not only possible. It is promised.

20 Keep my soul, and deliver me; Let me not be ashamed, for I put my trust in You. (Psalm 25:20)

Our willpower is not always on will call. We must decide today that we will no longer allow shame to be our filters to which we view life. But, we must view life through the lenses of truth wrought with humility and trust. You can tap into the power that will allow us to walk on top of the oceans of shame that previously were a source of drowning for me. This is how we walk on the oceans of shame. We trust the one who walked on water to carry us through this life in humility. We must trust him all the way. This is a path where ego (the greek pronoun "I") is replaced by eimi — (the greek verb "I am").

Repent & Fear God only

1 Have mercy upon me, O God, According to Your lovingkindness; According to the multitude of Your tender mercies, Blot out my transgressions. 2 Wash me thoroughly from my iniquity, And cleanse me from my sin. 3 For I acknowledge my transgressions, And my sin is always before me. 4 Against You, You only, have I sinned, And done this evil in Your sight— That You may be found just when You speak, And blameless when You judge. (Psalm 51:1-4)

28 And do not fear those who kill the body but cannot kill the soul. But rather fear Him who is able to destroy both soul and body in hell. 29 "Are not two sparrows sold for a copper coin? And not one of them falls to the ground apart from your Father's will. 30 "But the very hairs of your head are all numbered. 31 "Do not fear therefore; you are of more value than many sparrows. (Matthew 10:28-31)

The Point is not what God can do to you. It is who God is. Don't fear man who at his best can only take your life but fear God who can do much more damage to even your soul. Fear God or Fear man. It seems like a no brainer but we fear what man thinks. We want the approval of man. Jesus' words remind me that man can do nothing to you without the permission of God. The context suggests it is God's love for us that should cause us to conclude that He's the one to choose to please because he is perfect and perfect love casts out fear. Yes, He is all powerful but He loves us. Why fear man, unless we choose to believe that man truly deserves our loyalty, obedience and respect over God? What a shame, pun intended!

> *4 I prayed to the LORD, and he answered me. He freed me from all my fears. 5 Those who look to him for help will be radiant with joy; no <u>shadow of shame</u> will darken their faces. 6 In my desperation I prayed, and the LORD listened; He saved me from all my troubles. (Psalm 34:4-7 NLT)*

This is exactly what God did for me. He listened to me and saved me from my shame. He will do the exact same thing for you. As a result, I am a better, more confident person. My leadership has been immensely impacted by living more freely as the adopted son that God has called me to be. I do not want to take for granted that you are an adopted son or daughter of

God. There are four simple truths that you need to understand to believe and become His son or daughter.

(1) God loves You: (John 3:16; 1 John 4:8; Genesis 1:1, 1:26-27, Psalm 8:1-2, 19:1-4)

He created the world and everything in it for us to enjoy. He created you in His likeness and in His image to have dominion over the earth. What great love God has for us!

> *8 He who does not love does not know God, for God is love. 9 In this the love of God was manifested toward us, that God has sent His only begotten Son into the world, that we might live through Him. (1 John 4:8-9)*

(2) The original sin of Adam separated us (humanity) from the lover of our souls, God:

(Genesis 2:17, Genesis 3:1-8; Isaiah 59:2; Romans 3:23) I define sin as the selfish impulsive numb disposition we have at birth experienced in our rebellion against God and denial of the truth.

We then practice sin and appease our nature while at the same time dishonoring God. Sin must be punished by a righteous and holy God.

1 Behold, the LORD's hand is not shortened, That it cannot save; Nor His ear heavy, That it cannot hear. 2 But your iniquities have separated you from your God; And your sins have hidden [His] face from you, So that He will not hear. (Isaiah 59:1-2)

(3) Jesus, the Son of God Redeems us by exchanging His life on the Cross for ours: (John 3:16; Peter 3:18; Romans 5:8; 1 Corinthians 15:3-8) He is the only one who can forgive us of our sin. He took the punishment of our sin upon Himself. He suffered for us on the cross. He rose from the dead on the third day proving that He is God in human form and He is victorious over death. He can grant eternal life to those who believe.

For Christ also suffered once for sins, the just for the unjust, that He might bring us to God, being put to death in the flesh but made alive by the Spirit, (1 Peter 3:18)

(4) The choice is yours: (Romans 6:23; Romans 10:9-10) Choose eternal life! You need power from God in order to deal with the deep rooted issue of pride due to our sin. The choice is simple but a difficult one to make.

9 that if you confess with your mouth the Lord Jesus and believe in your heart that God has raised Him from the dead, you will be saved. 10 For with the heart one believes unto righteousness, and with the mouth confession is made unto salvation. 11 For the Scripture says, "Whoever believes on Him will not be put to shame."[fn] 12 For there is no distinction between Jew and Greek, for the same Lord over all is rich to *all who call upon Him. **13** For "whoever calls on the name of the LORD shall be saved." (Romans 10:9-10)*

You must empty your cup. Your cup is full of life experiences and teachings. You must empty your cup and start over only allowing the truth to be in your cup. We pour out from the cups of our hearts daily. What are the people around us receiving? We can share from the overflow of life in our cups. We can pour out and never run dry when we are drinking from a never ending fountain. Aren't you tired of living life out of your reserve tank? Through confession and repentance, allow God to empty your cup and fill it up over and over again. You must be willing to totally empty your cup to experience this freedom and healing. Empty your cup!

REFLECTION:

Have you placed all of your trust in God based on the finished work of Jesus? Why?

How would your life be different if there was no shame hindering you?

What do you want to believe about yourself that is hard to believe?

What is in your cup?

Conclusion:

Shame entered the world when Adam disobeyed God.

> *20 For when you were slaves of sin, you were free in regard to righteousness. 21 What fruit did you have then in the things of which you are now **ashamed**? For the end of those things is death. 22 But now having been set free from sin, and having become slaves of God, you have your fruit to holiness, and the end, everlasting life. 23 For the wages of sin is death, but the gift of God is eternal life in Christ Jesus our Lord. (Romans 6:20-23)*

Shame can be used to produce righteousness, however, for the sake of our journey, the shadow side or negative side of shame used to mask our true self has been our topic of study. From my experience, shame can lead to almost any one of the emotions mentioned earlier. Shame can lead to anger. Shame can lead to grief. Shame can lead to fear. Shame can even lead to an expression of happiness. Dealing with the core lies created by shame and developing new habits leads to freedom. I am trusting that by now, the mask has been at least identified and prayerfully removed. Several of us have on more than one mask, it may take more time. But it should not take 20 years as I have shared my journey with you. Use your reflections and apply the truth you have received from the Word of God to be set free. Find a wingman that you can trust. When you are looking to be vulnerable remember three things: (1) Communicate openly about your emotions. (2) Show empathy and active listening skills. (3) Share personal experiences

Conclusion:

to foster trust with those with whom you are sharing. You will never overcome shame by overcompensating with discipline. You must deal with the root cause. When shame is involved there is a great chance that you are not dealing with an authentic person. This person needs to understand who they are. They must strive to become the most authentic version of themselves. You will need help. The claim shame makes to us and about us is difficult to shake because the assertion comes from us and is validated by the world around us. You will need a true friend to show you what you may not be able to see. God asks the question with your best interest in mind. Who told you that you were naked? In other words, who lied to you? You need to arm your mind with what God says about you. Trusting in God and believing what He says about you is the cure for shame. He listened to me and saved me from my shame. He can do the exact same thing for you. Now I can walk on the oceans of my shame. It is now in my past. It is extremely important to be courageous in confronting shame and finding healing. I encourage you to embrace your own narrative and step into a life free from the shackles of shame. My final words of encouragement and empowerment are for you to continue your journey towards self-acceptance and living shamelessly. Time alone will not heal all wounds. However, in time after putting in much hard work, you will reap the benefits of selflessness, humility, accountability, mastery and endurance that lead to the rich rewards of self-awareness. You will experience true emotional healing. Today I am free from shame. I am able to make difficult decisions without the internal critic hounding me and telling me the odds. In the words of the STAR WARS character Hans Solo, "never tell me the odds!" I am at peace. I know who I am. I can walk on top of the waters of my shame and so can you. Your journey can begin now. I would love to hear how this book has helped you move toward freedom in your life? I wrote this book as a result of my freedom from shame. I can't wait to see what you will accomplish when you are totally free!

You will keep him in perfect peace, Whose mind is stayed on You, Because he <u>trusts</u> in You. (Isaiah 26:3)

The End.

Printed in the USA
CPSIA information can be obtained
at www.ICGtesting.com
CBHW042227110524
8331CB00008B/19